Last Poems

Last Poems

Doug May

Ober-Limbo Verlag

Acknowledgments

"Etagere," "Fathers And Sons" and "Binaries" were first published in *Cathexis Northwest.* "The Truce" first appeared in *North Dakota Quarterly* in a slightly different version. "Quarantine" and "Derby Day" appeared in *Sparks of Calliope.*

Published by Ober-Limbo Verlag
Heidelberg, Germany

ISBN: 978-87-971569-8-8

Cover photo, design and layout
by Birgit Stephenson

This book is dedicated to Henry Stanton with
deep appreciation for all the help and
encouragement he has given me and other
writers outside the mainstream.

And to Greg and Birgit, as always
To Karen, for tomorrow

Author's Note

These poems were written over a period of 40
years. No chronological order is implied.

This book is not intended to come after the
others. Which are not finished. Though maybe
completed.

It may or may not be the most recent in time. Or
the final item in a series.

It may even last. But last is not given.

Listen to the music of Morton Feldman for
additional possibilities....

CONTENTS

Afterhours (The Tattooed Bookkeeper)

A tech school graduate, smartly attired
Yet not adhering to the latest look,
She stays until the final debt's retired
And gain's recorded in her doomsday book—
Re-checking plugs and coffee pots before
She kills the lights. Dependable as smog,
She's only called in sick a time or two
And showed up late the day she hit a dog.

No one would guess that underneath her blouse
A dragon green as jade and red as phlox
Wraps claws around a hermit's bamboo house,
Or that she shows the night shift janitor
Its fleshy curves—the way a snake will share
The thrill of danger with a hungry mouse.

Quarantine

For years it nibbled at his tired routine:
The urge to book a fortnight at some inn
Beside the sea. An inspiration clean
As ice and bracing as a splash of gin
It kept returning like a melody
From vanished days until his brain
Looked forward to its questioning refrain.

But with each passing year he grew less sure
Of how to leave the house, compiling lists
Of things his settled ways could not endure
For long: the lumpy beds and drizzling mists
Of beige motels and plane connections missed—
Postponing the escape that none can stay
By snuggling deeper into yesterday.

The Loan

The frame sits half-completed on a lot
Where aging bungalow did not deserve
New Spanish tiles and marble countertops.
Sometimes a stranger will arrive by dusk
Seatbelted to an aging SUV
And survey half an acre's disarray
Encircled by perimeters of tape
Where kids played blind man's bluff or keepaway.

And as she listens to the sighing flute
Of traffic westward bound, she thinks how much
Depends on what somebody in a suit
Who measures risk against a moving chart
Decides about a name he's never met
While clearing hurdles for the next Walmart.

L.A. Hustle

He thought he wouldn't fit into the scene
In Hollywood unless he shed some weight
And dyed his hair Mars Black. By Halloween
He'd know enough about their fickle minds
To hire a looker at the going rate
To answer calls and tinker with the blinds.

But they were too consumed by ocean views
Or lining up their putts to hear his spiel
So now he cruised the palm-lined avenues
Of Santa Monica with three tight scripts—
A safer game than hedging's roulette wheel.

And anyway the swells owed him a trip
To Bel Air and a repo car that ran,
His name above the best boy's and the grip's
In lights—because he hadn't fought in Nam
To play a central casting also-ran.

Insurance Policy (Assisted Living Sketch)

In twenty years he hadn't cracked a smile.
His misery was often caused by food
Prepared in some exotic style
But also sports, music, politics and
Females—especially the bossy ones
Who did men's work. He didn't diet or fast
But walked each day—while worrying over
A face without a name from times long past.

He hadn't planned on reaching such an age
And barely understood the reason why
He paid an agent's strict unliving wage
When death refused him like a nervous bride
(Now that his brain could only juggle colds
And aches while letting distant kin decide.)

Valedictorian

He was the smartest kid in every class,
So smart that by 5th Grade he doubted God's
Existence and His sacred axioms
And corollaries that defied the odds.

But after he'd achieved straight A's and won
Admission to an ivied factory
His brain collapsed beneath the strain
Produced by algebraic geometry
(Which he found hard to understand as God
Instructing Abraham to kill his son)—

Expelled by reason's steady hand that served
Him faithfully, and exiled to a land
Of obscure prodigies and miracles
Demanding he obey, not understand.

The Curiosity Shop Window

He'll sell you knockoff jade or Chinese scarves
Stashed in a bygone yuletide's brownie tin,
No honest toil to smudge trimmed fingernails
Nor doubt to disconcert a smooth pink chin.

"Why anyone would want those things…" he snorts
At crazed Toscano trolls he'd meant to shelve
Beneath Apache Tears and treasure maps
Designed to fool grown men of ten or twelve.

Before his window homeless scroungers beg
From passersby too busy to reflect,
Their faces melting in the common blur
Of antiques weathered by unseen neglect

(While underneath his breath the shop clerk sniffs
That wino, thief or shirtless knockabout
Should not be left to spoil a track-lit view
Of pearls consigned to dust or just tossed out.)

At A Bar In Westwood

He said that the producer wouldn't reply
To his comment about the final scene
In Bonnie and Clyde. The one where bullets
Go ripping through the bandits' flesh with such
Rhythmic alacrity that they start to flail
Like puppets on strings, each sustained volley
Of buckshot lending their spasmodic waists
A supportive arm like a partner at a
Dance marathon. He said that they could have
Put music to it—horns and a synth—and
Started the next dance craze, the "Bonnie and Clyde."
He blamed his descent into alcoholism
On the producer who lived in the canyon
And all the rest who couldn't smell success

And his tall sorority-queen ex-wife
Who liked to dance with strangers at the bar.

Interrupted Signal Fire (The Fugitive)

We didn't realize how quick the trail
Could lose itself before the sun went down.
For hours we struggled past the gargoyle teeth
Of catclaw snares and cholla spines, each turn
Deceptive as a shaft of slanting light
Dissolving into wet green choruses
Of blackened earth. Had someone earlier
Refused to double back before nightfall
And—lost beyond a greenhorn's reckoning—
Felt wave upon slow wave of ancient fear
Engulf his mind's precarious repose?
A pile of twigs just barely scorched by flame
The sign of one who'd rather wander lost
Than face tomorrow's hanging sword of blame.

Obsessive Horticulturist

He was a doctor from Mumbai, well-versed
In brain scans and EEGs. An orderly and
Quiet fellow who'd always check his
Wall Street Journal in the morning and
Prune back in winter the yellow roses
That overflowed his Spanish patio.
He had a secret passion, however,
That caused him to forget sometimes his pose
Of polite detachment: mango trees. Whether
A blushing Haden or a Nom Doc Mai
Or Rubensesque Osteen with epidermis
Smoother than a Bombay courtesan's, he
Had to have them all. Until one day his wife
Swore that she'd dump him in the curry pot
    Beside a goat next time he borrowed from
    Their golden years to add a scion to his plot.

Still Life With Closet And Vacuums

They bump against the long-disabled blades
Of fans and frozen blenders yellow-tagged
For future lawn sales' early morning raids—

No longer threatening a Berber shag's
Mojave monochrome of ground-in grit
With vortex roar and yawning vacuum bag

Or choking on a moppet's stenciled knit
Beneath her bed's imaginary zoo
Where even lions and octopuses fit:

Retired veterans of the war between
A puppy's paws and those who grimly strive
To keep their temporary cages clean

Concealing rooms of orderly despair
By laundering death's footprint on the stair.

Gothic Tale (The Heretic)

One evening long ago, a common lout
With bulbous drunkard's nose and bunioned feet
Sank down upon decrepit knees to pray
Before the Father, Son and Paraclete—
Petitioning with zeal for them to slay
The Devil's company of fear and doubt.

While crouched beneath his sheets a cozy bug
Equipped with sturdy exoskeleton
And pincers threatening some awful doom
Prepared to navigate the coarse homespun
Belonging to this claustrophobic room
Ungraced by tapestry or damask rug.

Without a wizard's book of ancient lore
Suggesting where to chance upon a trail,
It slipped and stumbled over threads and grease
Unsteady as a sailor in a gale
Until propelled into a blanket's crease
By restless sleeper's cataclysmic snore.

Thus inconvenienced, it took a break
To set its curled appendages aright
By rocking busily from side to side
Before it won at last against the might
Of gravity and pricks of injured pride
To travel onward like a tool of fate.

The peasant stirred, his cauliflower ear
Annoyed by unintelligible words
That bounced from brittle bone to hardened wax
While scurrying earwig chased the prize ignored
By harvest scythe and roughhewn woodman's axe,
Urged on by curiosity and fear

Of what might seize him from the rear. Each move
Another unplanned reflex in a game
Played out without firm rules or well-lit court
Until at last exhaustedly it came
Upon the chemist's mystical retort
Invisible to commerce, art and love.

At dawn the sleeper cursed the sick malaise
That often took up quarters in his head
And staggered down a narrow village road
With shoulder harness powering a sled,
Ignoring hops and Riesling vines unmowed
Which Vogelweide once had cause to praise.

And in the marketplace observed dead squabs
And ptarmigans, their eyes like gems
In still-life harmony with salted fish
And grapes thrust lusciously from russet stems—
The sirens of each groaning hook or dish
Seducing bustling unwashed mobs.

Then suddenly among those smells and sights
He heard a nasal voice hurl down its curse
Against consumers sensibly enslaved—
And felt his lips obey commands perverse
Addressed to flesh accused by what it craved
Of seeking to ignore the Inward Light.

Stung by this impudence crude as a sneeze
Directed at their jugs and roasting pyres,
They sentenced him to die in flames
Alongside vanities that bred his ire,
His ashes scattered—never to be claimed
By prophets, anchorites or Manichees.

But as he twisted on the blackened stake,
No eyes observed a brown twig scurrying free
Of incandescent ropes and charred remains
To father obscure tests of purity
And man the cockpits of four haunted planes
Pronouncing judgment on the marketplace.

1985—2021

Derby Days

Lubricated Delta Taus on infield grass
Egg on their dates to flash the TV crews
While solid seconds float between starched tents
Of towering hats and cable interviews.

Far from the off-track bets and whispered touts
In dim seclusion wait the thoroughbreds
With grooms and stable cats to calm their bouts
Of nerves before the solemn post parade—
Their blinkered eyes indifferent to raw slits
Of blazing sun and viscous smears of rain

Where uncrowned champions must either catch
A second wind and triumph on the rail
Or stumble gamely down the final stretch,

Deaf to the painted crowd and pounding track,
The shingle of one dangling hoof askew
Beneath flawed bone's hereditary crack.

Etagere

Nearly a century ago it rode
By steamer from Le Havre and east by train
To where a porter's swaying buckboard sat
In freezing rain, awaiting crated props
Pried from the grasps of shuttered ateliers
And smuggled past the customs cops.

It must have piqued their curiosity
In Cedar Falls, where frivolous displays
Of fickle affluence were seldom seen
And even cottages strove to abide
Like main street shops or red-brick factories
Behind facades reserved and dignified.

A miracle of scalloped paint and brass
Applied to poplar steamed for seven days
And molded into curvatures and bays
Appareled in the foliage of a park
As reimagined by some artisan
Who didn't leave his tradesman's mark

It stands beside the flat screen HTV—
Pot belly illustrated with a scene
From Cupid's court, a startled dove
Escaping momentarily its fate
While on the lawn a vulgar cherub chokes
Inaudibly his fat indifferent mate.

The shelf above is home to faux Laliques
And whimsically positioned dolls procured
From kitschy catalogs or plucked from bins
At dollar stores where imitation fruits
And plastic vines moon effigies of Death
In papier mache toreador suits:

All members of that unacknowledged tribe
Ignored by arbiters of excellence
Whose fickle emperors and peasants rub
Immodest glaze within a common space
And shadows' peaks and vales of shared routine
Deflect sharp edges into soft embrace.

Fathers And Sons

Another Friday at the watering place
For rats grown weary of their endless race
(Excluding junior members lured by whiffs
Of musk-and-sandalwood emitting quiffs.)

While recollections of that awkward phase
Intrude upon their prideful wounded daze,
The old ones weigh some casual snub
Of rites attaching to their misty club

And wink at how initiates flout laws
In favor of a moment's fleeting cause—
Then toast lotharios who stalk the night
Before it yields to wisdom's mournful light.

Binaries

Among the Spanish tiles and ranch house bricks
He stoops to snugly lace his Wal-Mart shoes
And execute the usual stretching tricks,

Ignoring lush green feints of sunrise views
And chaste recessionals of stately lamps
Ethereal as fading Betelgeuse.

The neighbor fills a window sconce, her damp
Rebellious locks and throat once kissed by fools
And cynics, college beaus or fleshy gramps

Defiantly extol night's threatened reign
By pressing to a highball's muddled rim
Plump crescents of abandonment and shame.

As vacant balcony and tuneless scrim
Announce the dawn, she greets her dead,
He sets his jaw more resolutely grim

Before onrushing waves of infrared
Deny the shadow foes he runs against
And tender ghosts who crowd her empty bed.

An Editorial

In words of judges gay or straight
I only hear our times' mandate:
Tear down the veils of Freud and Weems
No chronicle is what it seems.

John Adams blushed at Franklin's eye
Trained fondly on a French girl's thigh
While Quincy Adams grinned at whores
Encamped behind Mount Vernon's doors.

Buchanan never stooped to wed
But showed a lad his poster bed;
Old Hickory would not be coy,
Called Rufus King his Nancy Boy.

When Andy Johnson shed fine clothes
To prance like Bacchus through straight rows
Of southern oaks, he was reviled
For tutoring the undefiled.

Ulysses Grant cared more for rum
Than any blue nosed matron's bum,
But Garfield set his mind to screw
And did it on an oaken pew.

Bedridden with a swollen ball
Fair Harding scoffed at Albert Fall,
No head of state so rutting hot
Till Jack deflowered Camelot.

The heights to which these men aspired
While in the depths of passion mired
Desert them in their twilight hours
Like memories of golden showers

Entrusting those of future days
To figure out who screws who pays.

Pruning Out (A Frosted Parody)

Uncertain whether now's the proper time
For cropping dead wood left behind in spring
By cirrostratus verdicts from on high,
I lift a pruning saw hung from a nail
And gently torque its wobbly nut against
A weathered stock. Above my graying head
Indecent sticks command the wastes where doves
And mockingbirds alight to sing, and buds
Will soon emerge from swollen nodes to feast
On longer days and restless skies.

I seldom prune unless an errant bough
Comes close to snapping power lines; a tree
Knows best the destination that it seeks
And how to get there, and there's fruit enough
To harvest without butchering the trunk
Or pruning back the laterals to splines.
So what's in these immodest splaying limbs
That makes me want to shyly intervene
Before they're spied by blushing shoots and buds
Emerging over tantalizing weeks?

Scarred trunks of veteran sycamores
That lose their summer foliage by design
Inspire no ancient fear that dormant sap
Might not remember to wake up in spring.
But when subtropic evergreens unsworn
To winter trance and urged by longer days
To trust their restless urgings to explore
Tease last year's rigid headstrong cellulose,
A frown of disapproval haunts the dance
Of blushing youth and overwintered age.

And though I don't feel duty-bound to hide
The past encased in bark beneath a tall
Cascade of acrobatic vines or blur
Old compromises with ornate facades
Or topiary sleights of hand, I'll prune
The rotten frameboards of abandoned nests
No longer fit to harbor fledgling broods
And feed a backyard chiminea's rolling flames—
Permitting callow green its slapdash sense
And rough incision rings their own defense.

The Truce

My two uncles, neither of my flesh and blood,
Sit after dinner and swap tales of the war,
Telling with voices and hands
What it was to go out into pure uncertainty
With only their hungering eyes to frighten death.
And before my gaze they are lean and beautiful again,
The one slightly older diving into a slit trench,
The younger one fear-struck at a stubborn frag
Hanging close to the bombardier's window.

There is a pause and the older one
Begins to tell of Anzio
And how each man dug himself a mouse hole,
Falling asleep until he woke or died.
Deep in the reaches of winter, someone saw his wife
Where the others saw only a pillar of sand
And he began to walk purposefully toward her.
Then when no one fired, this strange thing happened:
A truce was made and without saying a word
The two sides agreed that their common duties
Would take place in the open for a time.
And for several days within the heart of Anzio
These men cooked, gambled and swore—
Their backs turned, yet nearly touching
Until the Nissei Regiment came in one night,
Woke and saw Germans and began firing,
Rousing the others who made a lunge
To get free of what they hated:
Their own flesh suddenly grown foreign;
And the battle started fresh, the M1s drumming
All over the blood-mired sand...

The story ends, the rest of us held a moment
Like captives of a truce gradually released
To our precious wounds faltering in the dark,
Each of us unchanged by the knowledge
That on the cruel beachheads of our days
These moments come as they come, in which we
Do not relinquish the weapons of pride and gain
But bend a little closer to the simple waiting
In which we are brothers.

Later, after the guests have gone home,
I stand before the kitchen window and notice how
A group of men are standing by the redwood fence,
Appearing to lean slightly away from each other.
There are soldiers bivouacking and the yard
Now fills with them, bodies swaying against
Blazing green trees and voices moving in orderly columns.
They are the winners and losers going home into
The greater, undeclared truce of the earth,
But tonight they are resting here
Far from the din of any battle.
And they are real; the sound as of dry leaves burning
Is the noise of their smiles beginning to grow
In the spaces of dead campfires and scattered tents.

Low Average

They hide beneath a pile of socks and drawers
Among sex toys and lubricants unshared—
The first stamped with the State's official seal
The other certifying I'm impaired.

A GED insists I am no slouch
At imitating more accomplished minds
While every IQ test report confirms
That when it comes to solving cubes I'm blind.

Why does it matter? Now that it's so late
And like Popeye I'm fine with what I am?
A settled hash, too late to gnash my teeth
And wail against a rigged promotion's scam.

The simple truth is that I cheated, lied
And faked the answers that I didn't know
Because a grownup's pride could not accept
God meant my clock to run a little slow.

Menchildren

He is talking hard and fast
about his enemies
across the street
or behind the doors
of offices

and how rush hour traffic
makes him want to
ban the snowbirds
in their lane-hogging RVs

or knock the stuffing
out of a softball
at a church picnic
dreaming it's a
bureaucrat's skull.

He would like to
forget this place
where nothing
obeys his will—

not the price of gasoline
nor the crimped stream
balky as his mower's
crankshaft

and not the relatives
who pretend that he
doesn't exist.

Tonight he tells me
he's trying to decide

whether to grind
an autumn elk
into Thuringer

or split cordwood
and stack it neatly in ricks
the way his father
and grandfather did,

to keep the yard trim
and cupboard stocked
with bottled water
and cans of vegetables
organized by date

in case an asteroid
changes its mind.

Like him I've got
the yearning
for which there is
no cure.

And though I don't
cling so hard
to cannons snug
as bedtime toys

I share his need
for boyish
things

and heroes
belonging to
vanished boys.

A Violation

The neighbor
found him
in her bedroom
in broad daylight,

two suitcases
clenched in his hands
a pair of sneakers
laced around his neck.

Now her twisted face
keeps replaying
how he jumped
through the window
and over a wall

zig-zagging from
imaginary bloodhounds
and ghostly bullhorns.

The terrible part isn't
the wedding ring
but how he knows
the things she hid
from everyone,
even herself.

She is living in a cage
at the edge of
a dark woods

trying to remember
how it felt
before someone
without a name or a face

left her naked as a leaf
at the mercy
of the wind.

Hoarder

This afternoon
I found a handprint
of black spores
inside the stuffy
bedroom closet

and boxes of old
Shaded Dogs
and vintage
Columbias

stuck together
like dead leaves
in a swamp.

I decided to throw everything out
before the mold invaded
the air ducts.

but as I raised
the dumpster lid
I heard Albanese's
Un Bel Di
smooth as butterscotch

and Dave Brubeck pounding
blue steel girders
through sun-drenched fog.

And I started to cry
over the voices
of the dead

knowing I would lose
the unfinished
symphonies
they nursed

more precious than
fresh prisons
of closet space.

A Dear Old Couple (Divorcing At 90)

He kept wanting
to go for a walk
through the old neighborhood
where he'd been chased

by a bully
trying to steal
his mama's change
from the sock
beneath his hat.

This was before
the girl down the street
caught his eye
and everything
stopped—

the hum of wires
and pigeon gossip

the strangled bleat of
clarinet scales
from a 2nd story
apartment
when he saw her

and forgot all about
the neighbor bully and
finishing his errands
on time—

so why now?
why at 11:30
after the talk
show ended

with their scrappy
tendrils
still hitched
tightly as a
square knot.

when it's too late
to look both ways

and jump back
from the dry-humping
shadows and

pantomimes
of forgiveness

at the end
of an alley
80 years
long.

The Scapegoats

50 years later H-O-R-S-E
is spelled the same
and it still isn't kosher
to swish a letter

while the clumsy guy
with a broken shot
turns his back
to lace up a sneaker.

I told lies all the time
and diddled myself
beneath an acolyte's
stiff white frock

but I never felt
the devil
so close

as when hymie and kike
squatted like
venomous toads
on my tongue—

the gift of my father
and his father's father
generations of cheated
Midwesterners and their
silent resentments

like crumbling paint
on a garage wall
hidden behind
cheesecake pinups.

And for years
the children of
Moses and Abraham
stepped forward

when I needed
somebody to blame
for flunking algebra
or biology

or getting fired
after three days
on the job.

Then I woke up and
suddenly there weren't
any more Jews
volunteering to
take the rap

for the lost jobs
and mistaken
identities.

Not even gentiles
without faces
hiding behind
dummy corporations

and retreating
to satin coffins
with surgically
corrected fangs

five minutes
before dawn

(just a pin prick's
teeming red slum
where the future
was always written
in code

impersonal as
receding gums or
bad hands
in the outfield.)

Strangely Compatible

Like the ones before
she tried to be gentle

listen, I love you
like a friend

but I can't
make up stuff
because I'm sorry

or because
you want me
to lie.

After months of
crowding her
clumsily as a wino
on a rush hour bus

I decided to drive off
the edge of
Coal Mine Canyon

(but only made it
as far as Flagstaff
and the tattooed alley
behind the foreign car
garage.)

Later she roused
her lazy serpent fire
with the help of
Gopi Krishna

and a doctor told her
she was borderline

(the kind that means
you change into
somebody else

not the kind where
you guess
the wrong box.)

After she got better
she still needed me
to drive her around
or listen to her complain
about her boyfriend

showing her gratitude
by lying on the sofa
one afternoon
in a terrycloth robe

knees drawn up
and eyes booby-trapped
like peppermints
on a silver tray.

And when she rose
to shake out her hair
and have a smoke

I realized I'd never
wanted her deep down
in the jealous way
of a lover

but just to prove
I wasn't a mama's boy
being warned not to
go out on dates
or fall in love

because I wouldn't
be able to support
a wife and
family.

And suddenly
it didn't matter
that I wasn't
handsome or
smart in school

just two arms
skinny as tentpoles

a faded
angioma scar
on a flabby
white ass

a penis
too tiny to
circumcise
at birth.

And it became
our unspoken bargain
to live on that
airless desert
planet

sharing distances
of tacky tourist shops
and fumbled bribes

where borders
overlapped.

Record Shop

for Chrissy

Oh golden days of unexpected
and clumsily extended youth,
I miss that big flickering box
of neon and linoleum

where someone paid me to
peddle elevator jazz
and flirt with Florentine Madonnas
half my age—

the only place where
lawyers could argue
Jimmy Page or Hendrix
beneath neon guitars

and scraggly bikers
lobbied for Rheingold
on slow Friday nights.

I miss the cowboys and rappers
and emos in combat boots
swaying in a magazine aisle
to an urban backbeat

Mike And The Mechanics
on autoplay
every Christmas Eve

homeless shoplifters
stuffing anime porn
into camouflage rags—

screaming
go ahead
go ahead
just break my assets
and get me a lawyer

Wu Tang Clans and
Insane Clown Posses
rubbing shrink-wrap
with Celine Dion

mustard shopping bags
swallowing beer money
and child support.

How thrilling to
update a wish list
that always knows
what I want

how grateful to hear
the ring at the door
that means every day
is xmas.

No more Prairie State
Hawkeye State
Buffalo State
Beehive State

just the zero state
of postal zones and
flat rates

where hollow loaves
glide silently.

Temp

The first couple of days
nobody notices me
until a kid in a Gap shirt
with not enough
to do

says to go
help out with the
billing.

Then when I mess up
their books in strange
new ways
he orders me
to switch out

an air filter or
urinal block and
try to look happy

like I'm in
on the joke.

Everything's good for
awhile I'm there on
time in my
ordinary disguise

before suddenly it starts
to rain—I screw up
in ways I never did,
not even at job rehab

forgetting to
mop underneath the
reception desk

or dust the salesman's
framed ping pong
paddles.

When their eyes grow small
and hard as last week's
leftover
blueberry scones

they say, it's ok
we still love you
but we can't wait
for you to catch on

or pay for night classes
like you're part
of the family.

So out the door and on to
the next vinyl palm and
sawdust credenza

the next roach coach
twice a day

the directions
and routines
I repeat
in my sleep.

Becoming the parents
I never knew
clinging like popcorn
and burrito smells

to motel rooms
with no check-out time
but plenty of hot water.

Opportunity

The Polish baba candles eggs,
The nurse from Russia patches clocks,
The *chica in vacqueros* legs
A double shift inspecting socks
To earn *remesas* sent back home.

Becoming nervous citizens
Of cubicles and check-out lines
Exiled from blood-yoke's ancient caste
To gladly pay the hourly fine
For worshipping what doesn't last.

Card-carrying Americans
Condemned on restless nights to wake
From dreams and ponder why they fled
Ancestral mountainside or lake
Before wounds dried that never bled.

Europe And America

in Europe they socialize
life and death.

in America they socialize
football stadiums
and gambling debts.

One Hundred Years

this day would have begun
like all the others,

empty the bag of urine
crank up the pillowed
hospital bed

guide a flexstraw
between her clenched lips
until her eyes bulged
wide as a baby's.

sometimes she'd bite my
thumb when it was time
for her bath

and I'd make myself
count to ten
like she taught me
in 3rd grade

(when I wanted to hit
the bratty neighbor
for calling me a
teacher's pet

at the choo choo park
with the eskimo pies
and emerald
lagoons.)

now she's just
a soft dent
that still
feels warm

and the smell of
antique lace and
mothballs
that won't
go away.

Distant

We thought our grandparents
were cops who needed
to be bribed with
pecan logs and electric blankets
on Christmas morning.

Who knew what they
thought about the boy
behind the curve

and his quiet sister
with sun-bleached pigtails
and perfect scores?

When all they shared
were cobbler recipes
or long-winded tales
of the neighbor who'd
sprained his back

hauling a deer carcass
up a sill of black ice.

The place where they lived
dragged on like a sermon
because they didn't have
drive-ins or goofy golf,

just a few Blackfoot
cooks and lumberjacks
sleeping off binges
in pickup trucks.

A land cold and windswept
but less threatening than
the distance crowded into
a telephone wire.

The Church Lady (The Blue Balls)

I miss her deep voice
and cautious
smile

the slow words
encouraging me
to bring potato salad
or napkins
to the picnic

how she'd
edge forward
like a shadow
on the porch

still keeping
the proper
God's distance.

But most of all
I miss that sundrunk
winter afternoon
when she accidentally
bumped against
my knee

leaving two
soft gray stones
floating upside down
in an icy pond.

Depression

there is a pain
with no here
and no there.

it comes and goes
and never stays
long enough
to leave a clue.

like a getaway car
halfway in
halfway out
of the driveway

concealing a body
in the trunk.

Short Seller

when you're crazy
you see things that
aren't really there.

but when you're smart
you see things that
aren't really there
and turn them into
a big pile of money.

you do this
by telling everyone
how to get to
the surprise party

where the only one
who doesn't
bother showing up
is you.

Low Salt Diet

blind miners, bleached sailors,
crystalline caterers to
belly marchers and
tongue twizzlers.

you the last dash added
and first taste awakened,
a titanium highlight
crowning a red nose.

I understand now why
all the conquerors
taxed salt—even imperialists
raised on hardtack

and gruel know that
humans will betray
ancestors, land and pride
before they trade
the savory

for a year
or two
of virtue
salt-deprived.

Guilt

a mental health flight risk
I pay the bondsmen
every day

to tie my arms
and legs
to the bedposts

and burn me with
cigarettes.

and when they go home
at night and ask
the face in the
mirror

"why can't I hold on
to money or love?"

they feel my shadow
pushing against
their bones

stretching skin
tighter than
albatross wings.

even guilt
becomes infected
by guilt

a silent train
in a buried
tunnel

window panes
closing in like bats
with children's
faces.

Shaggy Dog

somebody's wife gets sick,
he tells God he'll clean the pigeon shit
off the statue of the priest
in the courtyard
if she recovers,

then she makes a miraculous
turn for the better
and he has to
keep his end
of the bargain.

while he's scrubbing the padre's
cement pedestal
somehow he hooks the arm
pointing toward heaven

and the statue falls and
smashes his leg
which has to be amputated
in an unsanitary
emergency ward.

afterwards he sues the church
for pollution and dies
from stress which all goes to prove

one bounce of intervention's
worth a thousand pounds of curé.

Relative Motion

it's better
not to have
a life.

then you don't
have to take
ownership

put up signs
train
watchdogs.

the safe bets
leave creases
in your forehead

the easy handfuls
crater your eyes
in bruised
aftershocks.

this is all
the evidence
you need

that a planet
moves
every time
you lie.

Tantrum

my crazy buddy,
two weeks
after he buys
the Honda he
decides he
doesn't want it
because he
accidentally
kicked a hole
in the floor board
when it didn't go
fast enough.
I told him
to show up
at the dealers
wearing only
an adult diaper
and threaten to
roll around
like a scalded dog
if they didn't
take it back—

hell, it always
worked for me
nobody wants to
watch some weird kid
who's taller than
the teacher
create a scene
in class

(whenever he
finds out his
extra credit projects
don't add up
to a promotion

and his sticky
brown nose
won't sway
the judges
who cut babies
in half)

Learning Without Remembering

nobody
uses the
guest room

except homeless
wayfarers
trying to keep warm
on a motheaten
sofa.

the pile of stones
in the back yard
keeps getting
larger

every time
I take another load
and dump it
in the pond.

but each newly
minted edge
shines with
a secret color

unblended
from primary
night.

The End Of The Summer Of Love

I'm just getting off
in some whistle stop
east of the Sierras
when the bus driver
asks me

"son, are you sure
you know where
you're going?"

and I point to
the party in the
rear view mirror
and act like
everything's OK.

I don't tell him
about the guy
in the next row
who has a bomb
taped to his chest

because I know
the words would
only melt into

refugee eyes
at an all night
laundromat

quickly forgotten
beneath detours.

everything's
a ten minute stop
on the way down
the mountain

a place to
share the old
waiting game

with passengers
I will never see again.

To The Righteous Politicians

who will love
the accident
with an uncertain
future?

who will loosen the squeaky
crumbs of sleep and
roll away the avalanche
of nails and shingles
anchoring his dull eyes?

not a mother
gone to market
not a daddy
drunk on the porch.

not God on a sheet
getting measured
for a fancy urn
over the fireplace.

Not Enough Information

I need to
understand
simple and
plain

whether
or not
to signal

from the
right turn
only
lane.

I want the cop
who needs
something
to do

to draw
me a map
big as
the world

and small as
a leftover
clue.

Tree Of Futility

my Indian Bael fruit
smuggled past
the whitefly squad

has managed once
more to shed
a lawnful
of skunky leaves
in July.

I know his new
flower buds
will incinerate
like moths
in a furnace

but I still feed him
wet black
worm castings

because I admire
how he yearns
like a vow of
silence

toward the perfect
unripened fruit
of hermits' caves.

**My Father, My Mother, Arguing About Money
Before I Was Born**

he said someday
there would be
bigger closets and
grander cupboards

even drapes
ordered out of a
mail order catalog

instead of rescued
from a barrel
of scraps.

but she said it's
now or never

a new mouth
can't live on
potato buds
and Monday
gravy.

first kill the
shaggy beasts
of food and rent

make yourself king
one island at a
time and quit

grabbing for the
magic ball of string
on nobody's
mainland.

Temptation

when I was walking
the dogs yesterday
I heard a young
boy's voice

"hey mister,
aren't you going
to kidnap me?"

and slouched against
a chain link fence
a dishwater blonde
skateboard prince
brown as a cinnamon
churro

stuck out his tongue
and dared me to look
a millisecond
longer.

off in the distance
I heard the chop and whir
of police helicopters

and cicada drone of a
microphone

put up your hands
we've got you
surrounded!

but all I could see
was a moonpie belly
winking through a hole
in his baseball shirt—

how did he know
I was still the weird
tall 6th grader
who liked to play
with younger kids?

that a lifetime of
keeping a safe distance
and doing the right thing

couldn't stop
a crooked grin
and fuzzy speck
of navel cheese

from unpeeling
the fishhook armor
of my raw green
center.

The Power Men

the power men crouch
in Rubbermaid buckets
with their chainsaws
and salsa radios.

they ask if they can cut
the tree limbs next to
the power transformer
they tell me there is
only one right answer.

they like to do this because
they are the power men
from the fast clean city
they like to do this because
they are the answer to why
things always happen
the way they do.

the trees smell frightened
their power lines sag
like tired grandmothers
rings of memories
come crashing to earth
dust-delayed.

everything happens for a reason
the long traffic lights
the gentle creep of fog
over silvery gray lawns

how long it takes me
to push a wooden sled
through traffic jams
of vanished buffalos.

Joyce, Faulkner, James

they always sound good
(though I know I'll have to
re-read every sentence
two or three times

even skip paragraphs
or whole chapters
in order to finish.)

afterwards I leave them
sprawled like heroines
on the sofa
or the carpet

wings stretched
and spines
broken

gold or tasseled
bookmarks
meant to impress
a book monitor

who never
shows up.

surely I was not meant
to understand
these directions
to a burning house

but turning their pages
fills my hands
with the soft wet kisses

and sandpaper tongues
of lovers without
scorecards.

The Ruling Class

silly fat iridescent pigeons,
you don't understand

why the bobwires
of the new
songbird station

want to keep you
from hogging all
the feed.

but that doesn't
stop you from
claiming its steeple
and noisily flapping
your wings

spooking nervous
sparrows and finches
wearing bellboy jackets

one lovebird
in a pink sherbet
tuxedo

and a thrasher
curmudgeon
sneaking a
craven
sideways
peek.

if you can't
have the birdseed,
you seem to
be saying

then
nobody can.

A Broken Hummingbird Egg

a speck of dust
became a
mummified
lizard

inside a
smashed
porcelain
thimble.

that all
the king's
men

couldn't
cobble
together

into a rainbow's
shabby
winter
coat.

riding hot
updrafts
of wine palm
bubbly.

Privilege

there will always be
a doctor or a
social worker to say
how nice it was
that I could play
the piano
and make paper
airplane poems
that nobody read.
they know when
I'm too far gone to
do my chores
I'll still have a roof
over my head
because I didn't
grow up in a
Sec 8 shooting
gallery or escape
a ghetto prep
with knife scars
fading slower than
paper cuts. strangers
with good bones
and degrees on the wall
will always show up
in time to stretch a
cold sliver of hope
over darkness and
keep me snarled in
clean white ropes
of starting over.

Armchair Philosopher

as he got older, his casual
conversation became more of a
studied enterprise.

he liked to illustrate
his points and conclusions
with slow inflections

vowels burnished to
flagon roundness
consonants tweaked to
pungent asperity.

in earlier times he was
thoughtful but less
rehearsed,
a quiet student of absurdity

who felt no need to untangle
the mysteries of existence.

Guessing

nobody has ever
asked me
my theory of
writing poetry.

but if they did
I would say,
thank you
very much

for making me
guess in the
dark.

because when
I'm sure
of the answer

that's when
it's always
wrong.

and when I wake
the brain
in my stomach

that's when
I swim blind
into Christmas
morning.

Requiem For Stella Lane

You were just the way to get from
3rd Avenue to Central,
The artery connecting childhood
To traffic jams and unpaid debts.

Beside your August blacktop
Crazy people sat in wheelchairs
Calling to strangers for help
Or placing low stakes bets

With Negro orderlies. Nobody
Knew that the first house
On the left belonged to a man
Who owned a dozen patents,

They only saw steel bars
In front of his windows
A flat brown lawn and a
No Solicitors sign.

Now the church academy for
Fast-tracked future CFOs
Has confiscated the shortcut
Belonging to rich and poor,

The street nobody noticed
Except when they used it
To connect their bedrooms
To a drive-thru liquor store.

They say: His Kingdom is of
This world, give us this land
For a bigger football field
And a brand new auditorium

And we will give you back
The covenant of progress.
They say anybody can still
Reach the future's blare and hum

Without bypassing carports
With Pontiacs on jack stands
Deflated wading pools and
Kmart mini-trampolines.

Soon enough a stucco wall
Will shield the rich children
In their polyester uniforms
From eyes marooned between

3rd Avenue and Central
In the dusty leftovers of
Vanished date and citrus groves
Zoned for creeping blight.

And 6 AM won't smell like
Day-old grease and hot asphalt
Pulling on a blind dog's leash
As it started to get light

And I floated like a balloon
From a dying father's bedside
Sickly with cards and flowers
Of a foregone conclusion

Down a street without a face
Just a shortcut connecting
Tree forts and tall green men
To four lanes of confusion.